50 GREAT TIPS

golf

QUICK FIXES TO IMPROVE YOUR GAME

50 GREAT TIPS

golf

QUICK FIXES TO IMPROVE YOUR GAME

LONDON • NEW YORK • MUNICH • MELBOURNE • DELHI

Project Editor Chris Stone
Designers Phil Gamble, Sharon Spencer
Production Editor Tony Phipps
Senior Production Controller Shane Higgins
Managing Editor Stephanie Farrow
Managing Art Editor Lee Griffiths
Reference Publisher Jonathan Metcalf
Art Director Bryn Walls

First published in Great Britain in 2008
by Dorling Kindersley Limited
80 Strand
London WC2R 0RL

A Penguin Company

2 4 6 8 10 9 7 5 3 1

A CIP catalogue record for this book is available from the British Library.

ISBN 978-1-4053-3440-2

Printed and bound in China by Leo Paper Products Ltd

See our complete catalogue at
www.dk.com

contents

I'm from the old school … Practising is how I learned the game. To practise and build a swing is a victory in itself

VIJAY SINGH

THE FUNDAMENTALS

forming
the grip

forming the grip

To assume the perfect neutral hold requires some careful application.

■ Start by letting your arms hang down free from tension, with your hands either side of the grip, palms facing one another.

■ Now feed the club into your left hand, so the club runs diagonally from the first joint of your forefinger up into the fleshy pad at the top of your palm. Close your fingers around the grip.

■ Your left thumb should rest on top of the grip, just right of centre. In a mirror, only two knuckles on your left hand should be visible to you.

■ To apply the right hand to the club, keep in mind the all-important palms-facing principle. Bring the right hand in towards the grip and wrap the fingers around it. The right hand should fit snugly on top of the left, the right thumb and forefinger forming a soft trigger around the grip.

ARMS HANGING, PALMS FACING

CLUB RUNS DIAGONALLY

TWO KNUCKLES ON SHOW

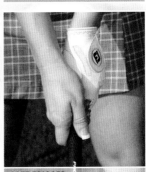
SOFT TRIGGER

02

THE FUNDAMENTALS

alignment

alignment

On the tee, good alignment is paramount. The principle of perfect aim and alignment could not be simpler. Imagine a railway track running down the fairway. The golf ball rests on the outer track, which points straight at the target. This is where you aim the clubface. The inner track runs parallel left of that target line. This is where you align your feet, hips, and shoulders. Collectively, this is known as perfect parallel alignment; it determines the path of your swing and is thus an essential requirement of powerful, straight driving.

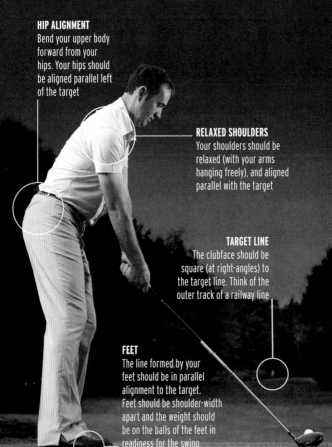

HIP ALIGNMENT
Bend your upper body forward from your hips. Your hips should be aligned parallel left of the target

RELAXED SHOULDERS
Your shoulders should be relaxed (with your arms hanging freely), and aligned parallel with the target

TARGET LINE
The clubface should be square (at right-angles) to the target line. Think of the outer track of a railway line

FEET
The line formed by your feet should be in parallel alignment to the target. Feet should be shoulder-width apart and the weight should be on the balls of the feet in readiness for the swing

03

perfect posture

perfect posture

To hit perfect drives, your feet should be shoulder-width apart with the toes splayed out slightly. The ideal ball position for the driver is opposite the inside of your left heel, as that encourages a sweeping angle of attack, striking the ball slightly on the upswing. The weight should slightly favour your back foot – a ratio of about 60/40 is about right. This primes you for a good weight shift into the right side in your backswing, essential for generating maximum power in your swing.

THE FOUNDATIONS OF A GOOD SWING

The driver swing generates the most power, so the need for good foundations is paramount. Balance and posture need to be perfect. Think "shoulders over toes, hands under the chin". That should help get your posture in great shape every time you set-up to hit a drive. Also, parallel alignment should be achieved; with the feet, hips, and shoulders all parallel to the target line. Good alignment promotes an on-line swing path.

FEET SHOULDER-WIDTH APART

04

ON THE TEE

*give yourself
time*

give yourself time

Don't be in a hurry to get to the top; just keep your rhythm and tempo nice and smooth. Give yourself time to make a good shoulder turn and, more importantly, time to complete your backswing. For the perfect combination of arm swing and body turn, think "turn your back on the target and point the club straight at the target".

KEEP RHYTHM SMOOTH

COIL THE SHOULDERS

SHIFT WEIGHT WITH THE CLUB

05

ON THE TEE

downswing and follow-through

downswing and follow-through

LET YOUR WEIGHT FLOW

Poor weight shift drains the power out of your swing like nothing else. The key thing to remember is that you should let the weight move in the direction of the swinging clubhead. So, as you swing the club back the weight moves on to your right foot; then as you swing the club down, the weight moves on to your left foot. Now you can punch your weight off the tee.

SWEEP THROUGH AND HOLD FINISH

Let the club swing through. Keep your head down until the right shoulder comes through and raises it naturally. The intention to complete the swing with a well-balanced finish has knock-on benefits for your entire swing. It instils in your mind the need to keep your balance, a key requirement of solid ball-striking. Also, in doing that, you are less inclined to lose control or hit at the ball less aggressively. The swing stays smooth, which helps promote a pure and solid hit.

FREEWHEEL

SWEEP AWAY

SWING THROUGH AND FINISH

06

the transition

the transition

Rehearse the transition in slow motion and practise it in front of a mirror: the weight shifts on to the left side, the hips start to unwind, the right elbow drops down to the right side, and the shoulders stay back. Try to ingrain this into your practice swings, until it starts to feel comfortable and you feel you can replicate it in your actual swing. Repetition is a wonderful thing. Practise this move to train good driving habits.

LEFT SHOULDER
As you start the downswing feel that you pull the left shoulder away from the chin

WEIGHT FORWARD
Keep your weight moving to the left as you swing into and through impact; do not under any circumstances allow yourself to fall backward away from the shot

WRIST ANGLE
Retain the angle in your wrists as this helps store power in your swing

STABLE BASE
Both feet should be planted as the downswing starts

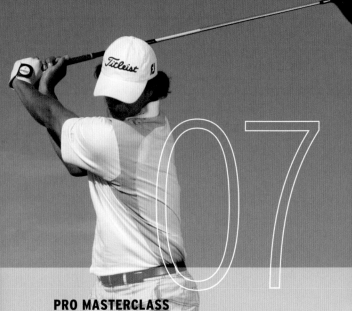

07

PRO MASTERCLASS

Adam Scott's shoulder turn

Adam Scott's shoulder turn

Adam Scott is not the strongest man in golf; he doesn't have the raw physical power of some bigger men on Tour. But he is a great driver of the golf ball, who has the ability to generate a lot of speed and distance, with good trajectory and a high level of consistency. A look at his PGA Tour statistics reveals that he hits the fairway almost 60 per cent of the time, and averages over 300 yards (274 meters) in driving distance. The position he achieves at the top of the backswing is picture perfect and it is one of the main reasons why he drives the ball so well.

Scott makes a full shoulder turn, winding his body up like a coiled spring. All the time, he is resisting with his lower body, the hips turning only half as much as the shoulders do. This action generates a lot of resistance – in essence, latent energy waiting to be unleashed.

From the top of the swing, he can then basically recoil his upper body – like a spring unwinding – which drives his downswing forward at pace. He converts all of that power into the back of the golf ball with a good hand and arm action.

Again, with Scott and the other big hitters, the secret is that the hands, arms, and body work together towards impact. One doesn't reach its target before the other, meaning that every part of the swing is well-coordinated and complements each other.

SCOTT'S FULL TURN GENERATES RESISTANCE

08

PRO MASTERCLASS

Vijay Singh's rhythm

Vijay Singh's rhythm

Rhythm in your golf swing is the key to consistent shot-making. Poor rhythm is debilitating with any club, but with a driver – the most unforgiving club in the bag – the effects are catastrophic. You will miss fairways, and lose balls, all day long.

Vijay Singh is a great scholar of the golf swing; and a man with a great swing himself. He advocates an old Bobby Jones adage, that you "start your downswing at the same speed as you took the club back".

It helps make smooth that crucial split-second transition from completing the backswing to starting the downswing. It gives you the time to coordinate the various moving parts in your swing, so that everything arrives at impact working in harmony. That is the essence of good timing. It is the way to hit drives long and straight, just like Vijay does.

SMOOTH TRANSITION

FAIRWAY METAL

static but
athletic posture

09

static but athletic posture

Your posture at address is integral to your chances of hitting a good shot because it determines the shape and quality of your body motion during the swing. It is easy to fall into bad habits, so when you practise, recreate perfect posture with this simple routine.

■ Stand up straight with your feet shoulder-width apart, your hands placed on the grip and your arms extended comfortably around chest height.

EXTEND ARMS

■ Bend over from the hips until the clubhead rests on the turf.

■ Flex your knees, feeling some athletic tension in the thighs. Try to feel that your back is relatively straight, and hold your chin high.

The golf swing is a fluid motion and it is hard to make a good start from a totally static position. Waggle the club back and forth as you prime yourself to start the swing; this helps to banish tension from the hands, arms, and shoulders.

BEND OVER FROM THE HIPS

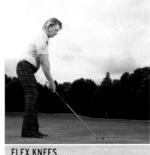

FLEX KNEES

10

V-FOIL

FAIRWAY METAL

left shoulder
over right knee

left shoulder over right knee

Starting from the address position, begin the takeaway. Your body motion is the engine of the golf swing. Your body needs to move correctly and efficiently in order to drive your swing. Think of turning your left shoulder over your right knee, to promote a full turn. And make sure you keep that right knee flexed, just as it was at address, as that gives you a firm base from which to wind and unwind your body in the swing.

SMOOTH TAKEAWAY

LEFT SHOULDER OVER RIGHT KNEE

11

V-FOIL

FAIRWAY METAL

full rotation

full rotation

As you swing your hands and arms through, the body needs to continue to unwind. The momentum of your swing will carry you through impact to a finish, but it helps if you think of completing your swing with your chest facing the target. This will get you "through the ball" better than ever.

UNCOIL THE SHOULDERS

ROTATE THROUGH

CHEST FACING TARGET

FAIRWAY METAL

perfect plane

perfect plane

There are several key checkpoints you can rehearse as you
practise hitting balls; this is one of the best. As your left arm
reaches parallel with the ground in the early stages of the
backswing, make sure that the wrists are fully hinged, thus
setting the club on the perfect plane.

   Check it in a mirror; your hands should be right in front of
your chest and the shaft of the club should be at an angle that
hits the ground roughly equidistant between the golf ball and
your toes. This is perfect plane. From there, you just keep
turning your shoulders to complete the backswing.

KEEP IT TOGETHER
Feel that the arms swing at the
same time as the body rotates

CHIN UP
Maintain your height, to make
room for that shoulder turn,
and keep your chin up

TURNING SHOULDERS
Turn your shoulders on a flat
plane to complete your swing

FLEXED KNEE
Maintain the
flex in your
right knee

KNEES AND HIPS
Let your left knee work towards
the ball as your hips turn

13

HYBRID SHOTS

hybrid from the rough

hybrid from the rough

SET-UP RULES

You can never ignore the set-up; it has a huge bearing on the quality of your shot-making. A poor set-up almost invariably leads to a poor shot; a good set-up massively improves your chances of making a good swing and hitting a solid golf shot.

When hitting a hybrid from the rough, move the ball a little further back in your stance than you would for a shot from the fairway or off the tee. Somewhere around two balls'-widths inside the left heel is perfect. Also, make sure that your hands are slightly in front of the golf ball. Combined, these two measures will help promote the slightly descending angle of attack that is necessary to generate good contact and a strong ball-flight.

THE PERFECT BLEND

A three-quarter backswing is more than enough for this type of shot – indeed it has its advantages in the sense that a compact swing is easier to control and can help deliver a crisp blow to the back of the ball. But you must complete that full shoulder turn, allied to the appropriate arm swing. To arrive at the ideal top-of-the-backswing position, think in terms of making a "flat shoulder turn and an upright arm swing".

PUNCH AND DRIVE

Hit down into the back of the ball, as though you're trying to hit a punch shot under the wind. This again reinforces the need, partly initiated in the nature of your set-up, to deliver a slightly descending strike. That helps make sure that the minimum amount of grass gets trapped between the clubface and the ball. It helps you make the best possible contact.

COMPACT SWING

DESCENDING STRIKE

DRIVE THROUGH

14

chip and run

chip and run

CHOKE DOWN AND SET YOUR HANDS HIGH

You need to pre-set a few changes in your set-up in order to execute the hybrid chip-and-run well. First, place the ball in the middle of your stance, with your weight slightly favouring your front foot. Secondly, choke down on the grip, almost to the metal – you want to avoid any wrist hinge with this shot.

Then stand as close to the ball as you comfortably can, with your hands a little higher than would be the case for a regular full shot.

CHOKE DOWN

ROCKING SHOULDERS

Now, you need to swing the club almost as you would a putter on a long-range putt across the green. Feel as though the stroke is controlled by a rocking motion of the shoulders combined with a simple arm swing. The hands should stay relatively passive in the stroke.

ROCK SHOULDERS

SWEEPING PATH

Executed correctly, you should find that the clubhead stays relatively low to the ground, back and through. You want to feel that the clubhead almost sweeps the ball on its way with a smoothly accelerating forward swing.

You should find that the ball is lofted gently forwards and, because there is no backspin generated at impact, it runs out towards the hole just like a putt.

You may find you over-hit the shot the first few times you play it, but with practice you'll soon find it is easy to judge distance.

SWEEP THROUGH

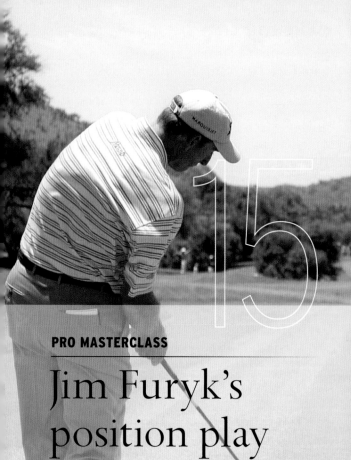

15

Jim Furyk's position play

Jim Furyk's position play

The fairway metal off the tee is a smart play; it gives you respectable distance and the extra loft on the face offers a greater level of accuracy than a driver. You can hit more fairways, which is a positive thing.

Once you've decided to hit a fairway metal off the tee, the key is to make sure you don't try to make up the distance that in the back of your mind you know you're losing through not hitting a driver. That's an easy mistake to make, but not one made by Jim Furyk.

Furyk's swing may not be picture-perfect, but there is no-one better at maintaining good rhythm and playing for position rather than for power. He believes in his swing, he knows exactly how far he hits the ball with that club, and he never pushes for more distance. That's why he hits more fairways than probably any other top player in the game.

So, when you're hitting a fairway metal off the tee, think position, not power. That's the whole point of the club.

THINK "POSITION, NOT POWER"

16

Paul Casey's wide arc

Paul Casey's wide arc

It is astonishing the distances England's Paul Casey can generate with every club in the bag. The fairway metal is no exception. This swing trait, however, disguises the real source of Casey's power. He sweeps the club away on a wide arc in the backswing and makes a superb upper-body rotation. It is a potent combination, one that any golfer would do well to try to emulate.

Relaxed hands, arms, and shoulders at address is a crucial starting point. Tension is a total killer. Casey then sweeps the club away low to the ground for the first 30in (76cm) and at the same time the left shoulder starts to turn in behind the golf ball. That's the first power move. From here the swing just flows.

SWEEP THE CLUB AWAY AND MAKE A FULL TURN

17

understanding
ball position

understanding ball position

Ball position is a fundamental aspect of iron play. Any confusion or lack of awareness of this part of the set-up can, and probably will, have dire consequences on the state of your approach play.

Here is a useful rule of thumb to work on. Play your wedge shots with the ball in the middle of your stance; then move the ball progressively further forward in your stance as the club gets longer. As a guide, the 5-iron is just over a ball's-width forward of centre; the 3-iron further forward still, inside your left heel.

The reason for doing this is that it helps encourage the correct angle of attack as the clubhead approaches the ball – relatively steep with the wedge and progressively more shallow as the club gets longer. It is one of the keys to solid iron play.

In terms of how far away from the ball you stand, again it depends on the club you are using. Quite simply, you stand progressively closer to the ball as the shaft of the club gets shorter. Use the posture drill at the start of the section of fairway metals to help you determine the distance you stand from the ball with every club in the bag.

BALL POSITION VARIES BY CLUB

CLUB LENGTH IS KEY

18

IRON PLAY

learn good
distance control

learn good distance control

Good distance control is the foundation of successful iron play. What you need to do is try to establish your own personal yardages for each club. Use your time on the practice ground to establish how far you hit each club – on the fly, that is – by hitting 20 balls and discarding the longest five and the shortest five. That middle cluster of 10 balls represents your average distance with that club. Write down a number for each club. When you're on the golf course, get into the habit of using a yardage chart. That professional approach will pay off. Then learn to control your swing.

Always make a smooth, well-balanced swing. You still need to commit to the shot through impact, but the overall motion of your swing must be within your own physical limits. Most top players swing at about 80-85 per cent of full power. It is the only way you can achieve the necessary consistency of strike and distance control.

PRACTICE WITH PURPOSE AND MAKE A SMOOTH SWING

19

make a full
follow-through

make a full follow-through

WRAP THE SHAFT AROUND YOUR NECK

Anyone who tells you that the follow-through makes no difference to the quality of your iron shots is missing the point. Of course, the ball is gone and on its way, but if you have in your mind's eye a positive image of how you want to finish the swing, you can improve the execution of your iron shots.

Here's a good image to have in mind. Wrap the shaft of the club around the back of your neck as part of a balanced finish to your swing. What this does is encourage a really positive release of the club into and through the ball. You'll hit consistently better iron shots as a result.

POISED FOLLOW-THROUGH

20

IRON PLAY

hands lead
the clubhead

hands lead the clubhead

It's common for many amateurs to flick at the ball with their iron shots, in the belief that this will help the ball into the air and lead to better shots. It doesn't; it's one of the worst faults in the game.

Look at the top players. Their hands lead the clubhead into the ball, generating a downward angle of attack. The key aspect to have in mind is making sure that there is a degree of forward lean in the shaft at the moment of impact. This compresses the golf ball, and means that your shots will have a much more effective trajectory.

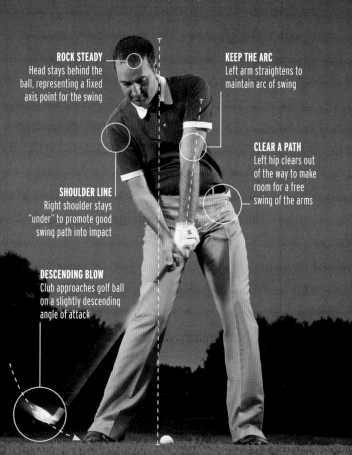

ROCK STEADY
Head stays behind the ball, representing a fixed axis point for the swing

KEEP THE ARC
Left arm straightens to maintain arc of swing

CLEAR A PATH
Left hip clears out of the way to make room for a free swing of the arms

SHOULDER LINE
Right shoulder stays "under" to promote good swing path into impact

DESCENDING BLOW
Club approaches golf ball on a slightly descending angle of attack

IRON PLAY

how to hit
a draw

how to hit a draw

Shaping a draw involves moving the ball through the air from right to left for the right-hander and left to right for the left-hander.

- Aim the clubface straight at the target, as if you are hitting a straight shot. Then align your feet in the direction that you want your ball to start off, without adjusting the clubhead.
- Now make a normal backswing following the line of your feet.
- Through the hitting area pay extra attention to rolling your right hand over your left to encourage a good release of the clubhead.
- Then follow through to a well-balanced finish.

The opposing angles at address, and the resulting path of attack and clubface positioning at impact, impart the necessary sidespin and cause the ball to start off in one direction and curve away through the air.

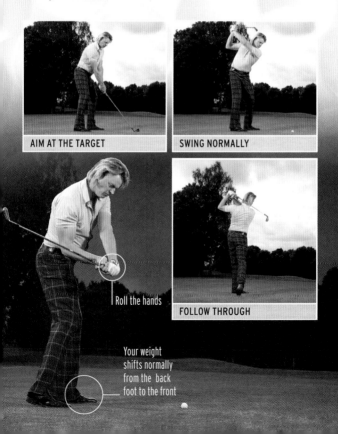

AIM AT THE TARGET

SWING NORMALLY

Roll the hands

FOLLOW THROUGH

Your weight shifts normally from the back foot to the front

22

IRON PLAY

how to hit
a fade

how to hit a fade

Hitting a fade involves moving the ball through the air from left to right for the right-hander and right to left for the left-hander.

■ Aim the clubface where you want the ball to finish – that is, straight at the target. Then align your feet in the direction you want the ball to start, while maintaining the position of the clubhead.

■ Then make a normal swing along your aim lines.

■ As you approach impact, delay the release of your hands – the opposite of rolling your hands, shown above – to make sure that the face stays open through the hitting area.

■ Proceed with your follow-through to a balanced finish.

With this shot and the draw, the key is to practise it enough that you can control the amount of movement through the air. Your ultimate aim is to be able to shape the ball to suit different situations.

AIM AT THE TARGET

SWING NORMALLY

Make your usual full body turn

DELAY THE HANDS

HOLD YOUR FINISH

PRO MASTERCLASS

Ernie Els's extended arms

Ernie Els's extended arms

Ernie Els is one of the greatest ball-strikers in the game, his seemingly effortless and beautifully rhythmic swing disguising serious power and great compression of the golf ball at impact. It's one of the many reasons why his iron shots fly so pure, straight, and far.

There is much in Ernie's swing that every golfer can learn from, such as the way his arms are fully extended as he swings the clubhead into and through the ball. This helps him carry good speed into the ball and deliver that all-important descending blow.

To emulate Ernie's positive move through impact, visualize your right arm extending fully towards the target and the clubhead travelling low to the ground after the ball. This will encourage you to swing freely through the ball; and extend your arms like Ernie does.

The right arm should be fully extended through impact

Keep the clubhead online with the target through the shot

The legs provide a solid platform for the powerful unwinding of the body and a free swing of the arms

EXTEND ARMS TOWARDS THE TARGET

PRO-MASTERCLASS

Colin Montgomerie's control

Colin Montgomerie's control

Scotland's Colin Montgomerie, a record-breaking eight-time winner of the European Tour's Order of Merit, may not have the most conventional-looking golf swing, but no-one in the modern era could be said to have better controlled the distance of their iron shots into greens. Monty has hit the ball pin-high probably more times than any golfer in the last 20 years.

One of Monty's great strengths, which is something which every amateur or club golfer can easily carry into their own game, is the way his swing maintains its rhythm no matter which club he is using, from the 3-iron to the 9-iron. And, specifically, the way he maintains the same rhythm in that crucial transition from finishing his backswing to starting his downswing. He doesn't snatch the club down. He gives himself time. Therein lies a lesson for every golfer. Keep that first move down silky-smooth.

KEEP THE SWING SILKY-SMOOTH

25

how to hit it high

how to hit it high

Hitting a high ball is probably not a shot you'll need to call on all that frequently. But if you have an obstruction in your way, such as a tree, or you need to attack a very tight pin position over a bunker, this is a useful shot to know.

Drastic changes to the set-up and swing are not advisable. It is far better in this case to keep things subtle.

■ You need a higher-than-normal ball flight, so it is necessary to pre-set a little more loft on the clubface at address by positioning the ball further forward in the stance. And rather than the hands being ahead of the ball, as was the case with the low shot, this time place them level with the ball.

■ Now make a slightly more upright backswing, getting the hands high at the top.

■ The feeling through impact is of staying behind the ball, your weight just hanging on the right side a fraction longer than normal.

■ With the ball on its way, proceed through to a well-balanced finish with the weight slightly more on the right side than usual.

Hands are level with the ball at address

BALL FORWARD, HANDS BACK

GET THE HANDS HIGH

HOLD YOUR WEIGHT BACK

BALANCED FINISH

26

how to hit
it low

how to hit it low

For the low shot, where you need to keep the ball under an obstacle, such as a tree branch, a couple of adjustments at address are essential.

■ To begin with, choke down on the grip an inch or two. Place the ball further back in your stance and hold your hands ahead of the ball; this de-lofts the clubface. You are effectively pre-setting a lower-than-normal ball flight. Place extra weight on your front foot.

■ There is no need to make fancy moves in your swing. Make a three-quarter length backswing, with a full shoulder turn.

■ In the downswing, try to feel as though your chest "covers" the ball through the hitting area. You should drive the club through low to the ground, with your hands very much ahead of the point of impact. Cultivate a sense that the clubhead stays low to the ground through the ball.

■ The abbreviated follow-through is a sign of a controlled, well-balanced, and punchy swing.

Do not be tempted to hit the ball harder. Just hit it better. Dead-solid contact is the real key with this shot. Remember, a lower ball flight will result in extra run of the ball upon landing, so allow for this when choosing your club.

BALL BACK, WEIGHT FORWARD

ABBREVIATED BACKSWING

STAY BACK

PUNCHY FOLLOW-THROUGH

PROBLEM SHOTS

ball above
your feet

ball above your feet

The first thing to understand when the ball lies above the level of your feet is that you'll have a tendency to pull the ball down the slope. There are a few swing changes to adopt to compensate for this.

■ Firstly, aim to the right of your target. Then, choke down on the grip. This shortens the club and thus compensates for the fact that the ball is effectively higher than it would be on a level lie. Also, stand a little more upright with slightly less knee flex.

■ The combined effects of the slope and the nature of your stance will encourage a slightly more rounded swing plane – the feeling being that you are swinging the club more around your body. That's how it should feel; just try to maintain your original height and spine angle as best you can.

■ Then rotate your body through to a finish, all the while maintaining your balance.

AIM RIGHT, CHOKE DOWN

Maintain solid foundations through the swing

MAINTAIN YOUR HEIGHT

KEEP YOUR BALANCE

28

PROBLEM SHOTS

ball below
your feet

ball below your feet

As the slope will influence the ball flight, you must accept that your stance and the awkward nature of this lie will tend to limit your body rotation.

■ The ball will tend to fly right, so aim to the left of the target. At address, bend from the hips more than you would normally, to get yourself down to the level of the ball. Plenty of knee flex is also advisable, as is a wider stance, to give you more stability.

■ Due to your inhibited turn, your backswing will be more arms-dominated, and therefore shorter and more upright. You'll generate less power, so club-up accordingly, and maintain a nice smooth rhythm.

■ Swing through as freely as possible within the confines of the slope.

The key to this shot is maintaining your original height and spine angle until the ball is struck. Any tendency to gain height, an easy mistake given the nature of the situation, will result in a topped or thinned shot.

AIM LEFT, BEND KNEES AND HIPS

Grip the club towards the end of the shaft

SHORTER, UPRIGHT SWING

FREE FOLLOW-THROUGH

29

ball on an upslope

ball on an upslope

This is probably the easiest of all the shots from sloping lies, because there's a sense of being able to launch the ball into the air. However, there are a few ways to make sure you play it well.

■ Your right shoulder should be markedly lower than your left and your weight favouring the back foot. Adopt a slightly wider stance and aim right of the target, because the ball tends to hook from an upslope.

■ Try to swing in harmony with the slope and maintain your balance. Do not get thrown back onto your right foot, or lean into the slope.

■ Keep your weight stable and your head down through impact. Let the natural momentum of your swing pull you into the finish position.

ALIGN SHOULDERS WITH SLOPE

Steady backswing works in harmony with the slope

MAINTAIN YOUR BALANCE

KEEP YOUR HEAD DOWN

30

PROBLEM SHOTS

ball on a downslope

ball on a downslope

This is the toughest of all the sloping lies, because the downslope gives you the sense that it is very difficult to get the ball airborne. It is not imagined. The nature of a downslope means that you are deprived of loft, and it is all too easy to scuttle the ball straight along the ground.

■ Make sure your shoulders and hips are as close to parallel with the slope as possible – your left shoulder feeling lower than the right. Place the ball back in your stance. This is a very important point. You will tend to want to put the ball forward in your stance, as it feels natural to generate some elevation from there, but this will prevent you from getting the ball airborne.

■ Pick the club up a little steeper in your backswing with an early wrist hinge. This sets the club in a position from which you can more easily generate the necessary steep angle of attack into impact. Make sure you maintain your weight distribution all the way to the top of the backswing.

■ As you swing down into impact, try to feel as though you are chasing after the ball down the slope, staying well down through impact so that the clubhead follows the contours of the ground. Never try to help the ball into the air.

STAY DOWN THROUGH IMPACT

BALL BACK IN STANCE

EARLY WRIST HINGE

Try your best to maintain your balance throughout the swing

31

use the wind,
don't fight it

use the wind, don't fight it

The wind is an ever-present challenge virtually every time you play golf. And whether it is merely a gentle breeze or a strong and gusting wind, you have to know how to play it.

Playing into the wind you should take a bigger club and swing it easier; the ball flight will penetrate the wind far more effectively. Don't make the common mistake of taking the same club and just trying to hit it harder, as that never works.

When playing downwind, take less club and again swing easier. Don't take the same club and try to ease up on the shot; you will probably miss-hit it. Also, consider taking a 3-wood off the tee, rather than a driver. The extra height will allow you to benefit more from the tailwind and thus gain distance.

Playing with a crosswind, tour professionals will often work shots into the wind – for instance, hit a draw into a left-to-right wind – as they feel it gives them more control over distance and spin. This is the advanced option. Most times, however, it is easier to use the wind, rather than fight it. In a right-to-left wind, simply shift your aim focus to the right of target. Then hit a straight shot and let the wind do the rest for you.

AIM RIGHT

USE THE CROSSWIND

32

PROBLEM SHOTS

the long
bunker shot

the long bunker shot

Rule number one from any fairway bunker is to take a club with sufficient loft to clear the front lip. If it so happens that the club has the distance to also reach the green, consider that a bonus. Clean contact is everything with this shot, because sand soaks up the energy in the swing and therefore even slightly heavy contact results in catastrophic loss of distance.

SHORTEN THE CLUB

- Choke down on the grip about an inch. This will hold the clubhead up off the sand and help to promote a clean contact with the ball.
- Shuffle your feet into the sand to give yourself a secure footing. This will lower the base of your swing, so choking down on the club is key.

- Make a smooth, well-balanced swing and make sure you hit down into the back of the ball, rather than trying to help it into the air.
- You should strike the back of the ball, rather than the sand. If you catch the sand before the ball, it will feel "heavy".

SHUFFLE DOWN

STRIKE THE BALL FIRST

A secure footing will enable you to make a balanced swing

MAKE A SMOOTH SWING

33

PITCHING AND CHIPPING

four set-up
essentials

four set-up essentials

Poor-quality pitching often stems from a poor set-up. Here are
four steps to a better set-up and more successful pitching action.

■ Make sure that your feet are only slightly open, and that your
shoulders are square.

■ Choke down on the grip. This gives you maximum feel and
clubhead control as you swing.

■ Put the ball back in your stance and hold your hands forward.

■ Keep your chin up. This simple move tends to lead to a better
posture, with the spine angle more erect, and it gives you space
under your chin to turn your left shoulder. Try to feel as though
you are almost looking down your nose at the golf ball.

SET-UP IS KEY TO SUCCESS

34

PITCHING AND CHIPPING

crisp contact

crisp contact

The ideal pitch shot is one where the ball rises steeply to the top of its flight and then lands softly with little or no run. With this in mind, on the downswing you should encourage a slightly descending angle of attack. The goal is crisp, ball-turf contact and lots of backspin. However, you must not quit on the shot at impact; this will result in too large a divot and a loss of distance. Instead stay focused on making a positive swing through the ball to a neat finish.

ANGLE OF ATTACK

HIT THROUGH

MAKE CRISP BALL-TURF CONTACT

35

PITCHING AND CHIPPING

shoulder-to-shoulder swing

shoulder-to-shoulder swing

One of the most common mistakes that amateurs make when hitting pitch shots is to make a full swing and try to hit the ball too hard. The ball tends to balloon into the air, with no control of spin or trajectory.

Remember, pitch shots are all about control. It's not a contest of how far you can hit it. So, think in terms of making a "shoulder-to-shoulder swing". That is, the hands travel to shoulder-height in the backswing and shoulder-height in the follow-through.

Your only other focus should be on maintaining a smooth rhythm in your downswing and a sense of "natural acceleration" into and through impact. This encourages a sweet and consistent strike, making it easier for you to judge line, length, and spin.

SHAFT ANGLE
Take the club back just beyond the vertical position

HANDS AND CHEST
To help promote a synchronized golf swing, think of the hands staying in front of the chest throughout

LOW HANDS
The hands swing to shoulder height in the backswing, then through to shoulder-height in the follow-through

BODY ROTATION
Body rotates in harmony with the arm swing

NARROW STANCE
Legs are only slightly apart, creating a narrow stance

PRO MASTERCLASS

Luke Donald's open clubface

Luke Donald's open clubface

On most pitch shots, it is advisable to adopt a slightly open clubface at address. The reason being, it is easier to control your ball-flight and have some finesse in your game if there is some loft on the clubface. Also, it allows you to commit to striking down and through the shot, without the fear of over-shooting the green.

Look at a great pitcher of the ball, someone like England's Luke Donald. His swing is blessed with a wonderful sense of rhythm and timing right through the bag. And it doesn't matter if he is pitching from 80 yards (73 metres) or half that distance, he always commits to the shot fully through impact.

Keep in mind that it is not a hard hit; rather, a positive and committed strike delivered with a sense of the arms and body working together. It is controlled.

Keep a firm left arm through impact

Hands lead the clubhead into the ball

Focus on the back of the ball for solid ball-turf contact

COMMIT TO THE SHOT FULLY THROUGH IMPACT

3 7

PITCHING AND CHIPPING

chipping
set-up rules

chipping set-up rules

BALL BACK, HANDS FORWARD

It is an oversimplification to say that bad chipping always stems from a bad set-up. But it is certainly true to say that a lot of golfers make life extremely difficult for themselves by neglecting this important aspect of the chip shot.

The correct set-up for 99 per cent of all chip shots can be expressed in one simple sentence "ball back, hands and weight forward". This promotes a shape of swing that makes the clubhead approach the ball on a slightly descending angle of attack, leading to crisp ball-turf contact.

CLUB SELECTION

The set-up and the simple swing required to hit neat chip shots can be applied to different clubs. When you need to play a chip to carry some rough or a bunker between you and the flag - go with lots of loft, such as a wedge. If a low-running chip shot is required, go with less loft - a 7- or 8-iron. The swing stays the same. All you have to do is make sure that in your set-up the ball is back and your hands and weight are forward, and that your hands lead the clubhead into the ball. Trust your swing and just let the loft do the rest.

USE A WEDGE FOR LOFT

USE A 7- OR 8-IRON FOR RUN

38

chipping techniques

chipping techniques

HOLD HANDS FORWARD

One of the golden rules of chipping is to make sure that the hands
lead the clubhead through the hitting area, thus guaranteeing
that all-important descending angle of attack. That is a crucial
point of understanding for amateur golfers; if the hands stay
ahead, a clean and consistent strike is far more likely. If, however,
you allow the clubhead to overtake the hands coming into impact,
the arc of the swing effectively bottoms-out before it reaches the
golf ball. In that instance, a miss-hit is virtually assured.

KEEP FOREARMS SOFT

As you may have learned from previous tips in this book, any
tension in your hands, arms, or body destroys your chances
of hitting solid, consistent golf shots. This is also the case with
chipping. To prevent this insidious fault creeping into your action,
try to make sure your forearms stay soft as you swing the club
back and through. That thought alone effectively "oils" the swing
with a lovely smooth rhythm. It also helps to keep the acceleration
smooth through the hitting area, so that the ball comes off the
face not too "hot", but on a soft and easily controllable ball flight.

HANDS LEAD THE CLUBHEAD

DESCENDING ANGLE OF ATTACK

KEEP THE FOREARMS SOFT

MAINTAIN AN "OILY" RHYTHM

39

PITCHING AND CHIPPING

turn your body

turn your body

The typical chip shot involves a relatively short swing, but that doesn't mean to say that the body can stop working. Indeed, poor contact with the ball is often the result of the body not turning as the arms swing down, which often causes the clubhead to overtake the hands. So always think of turning your chest back and through in harmony with your arm swing. This gives the swing some nice momentum and, providing you keep your hands in front of the ball, helps keep the club on the correct downward angle of attack.

HEAD POSITION
Head only comes up long after the ball is on its way

UPPER BODY MOVEMENT
Hands, arms, and torso should work as a unit, turning together

SOFT GRIP
Grip pressure remains soft, for maximum feel

FLEXED
Adopt a narrow stance with flexed knees

FOLLOW-THROUGH
Clubhead travels through further than it travelled in the backswing

LOW CLUB
Clubhead stays low to the ground through impact and rises only at the end of the swing

40

PRO MASTERCLASS

Seve Ballesteros's improvization

Seve Ballesteros's improvization

Seve Ballesteros was the most creative golfer of his generation and he also had by far the best short game. These two qualities are inextricably linked. A good imagination is a pre-requisite of a successful short game. You first have to be able to visualize different chip shots around the green and then develop the touch and feel to turn those shots into reality. Chipping is not a one-dimensional affair. It demands variety.

So, always practise your short game with a selection of clubs by your side and make sure you constantly vary your target from one shot to the next. Each time, visualize in your mind's-eye the flight of the golf ball: where you want it to land; how much run is required to get it close to the hole. Remember, every shot is different. Once you have a picture in your mind of the shot you want to play, select the club that best performs that function. The key is to change the club to vary the shots that you play – some high with very little run; others low with lots of run.

Never stand by the side of the practice green and simply hit the same shot to the same target for long periods – there is no real challenge in that – and thus your short game won't benefit in any meaningful fashion.

WINNING DEMANDS IMAGINATIVE PLAY

41

adopt an
open set-up

adopt an open set-up

In order for you to utilize the bounce-effect of the sand-wedge, you must adhere to a couple of simple set-up rules that will affect the shape of the swing.

▦ The stance must be open – that is, the feet aligned to the left of the target.

▦ The clubface must be open – that is, aimed to the right of the target.

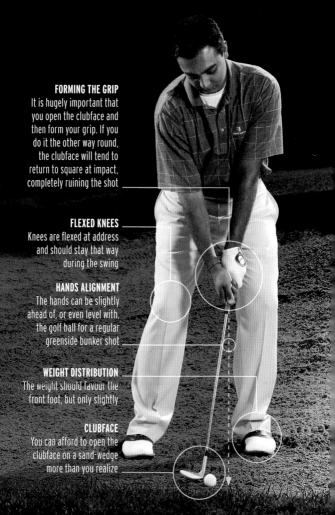

FORMING THE GRIP
It is hugely important that you open the clubface and then form your grip. If you do it the other way round, the clubface will tend to return to square at impact, completely ruining the shot

FLEXED KNEES
Knees are flexed at address and should stay that way during the swing

HANDS ALIGNMENT
The hands can be slightly ahead of, or even level with, the golf ball for a regular greenside bunker shot

WEIGHT DISTRIBUTION
The weight should favour the front foot, but only slightly

CLUBFACE
You can afford to open the clubface on a sand-wedge more than you realize

42

BUNKER PLAY

swing along
your aim lines

swing along your aim lines

By addressing the ball correctly, the swing becomes immeasurably easier. The secret is to swing along the lines of your body – in other words, across the line on an "out-to-in" path.

■ Focus on a spot in the sand roughly 2in (5cm) behind the ball; this is the intended point of entry for the clubhead.

■ Swing back and through, combining your arm swing with your body turn.

■ Strike down into the sand on your intended spot and accelerate the club through the sand under the ball, with the feeling of swinging the club to the left of the target through impact.

■ Always follow through on every bunker shot.

SWING ALONG YOUR AIM LINES

STRIKE THE SAND FIRST

REMEMBER TO FOLLOW THROUGH

Phil Mickelson's wrist hinge

Phil Mickelson's wrist hinge

Phil Mickelson has probably the most creative short game of any player at the top of the game and can produce a range of magical shots from around the green, including bunker shots. Mickelson often carries an exceptionally lofted sand-wedge, often as much as 64-degrees, and uses this to generate greenside bunker shots where the ball climbs almost vertically skywards and stops abruptly on landing. It isn't all down to the equipment he uses, though. The skill is in the hands, too.

He hinges the wrists early in the takeaway to set the club on a very steep angle of attack; this in effect pre-sets a swing arc that is distinctly U-shape in profile. The club therefore goes back steeply and then comes down steeply too. Mickelson then zips the clubhead through the sand under the ball with a fast and aggressive hand action; that's the key, fast hands through the ball. The ball pops straight up in the air and stops virtually dead in its tracks. This is a shot to practise before attempting it on the course.

USE FAST, AGGRESSIVE HAND ACTION THROUGH THE BALL

44

PUTTING

eyes over
the ball

eyes over the ball

Ball position is as important in the putting stroke as it is in the full swing. There are two factors to bear in mind. Firstly, the ball should be forward in your stance to encourage a slight ascending blow when the putter-face meets the ball. That imparts a good roll on your putts. Secondly, your eyes should ideally be directly over the ball, as this gives you the best perspective of the line from the ball to the hole.

One simple routine helps give you the perfect ball position. Adopt a comfortable posture and then drop a golf ball from the bridge of your nose. The spot on which it lands represents perfect ball position for you.

DROP A BALL FROM YOUR NOSE

PERFECT BALL POSITION

45

PUTTING

keep your
head still

keep your head still

Any head movement before the ball is struck knocks the shoulders – and therefore the putter – out of its natural path; this leads to a crooked stroke and a missed putt. It is particularly common (and damaging) on short putts, where there is a tendency for golfers to take an anxious peek and see if the ball is heading towards the hole.

One of the key objectives for any good putter, therefore, must be to keep the head rock-still throughout the stroke. The simplest way to achieve this is to commit to keeping your head down until you hear the sound of the ball dropping in the hole.

KEEP STEADY
The head stays rock-steady until the ball is on its way

MAINTAIN THE UNIT
A slightly fatter-than-standard grip is popular with many top players, as it tends to help keep the hands and wrists "quieter" during the stroke

NO MOVEMENT
From the waist down, everything stays still during the stroke. Imagine your legs are set in concrete

KEEP ON TRACK
From short range, imagine the face of the putter looks at the hole through impact

SOLID BASE
Your weight should be evenly spread between both feet, with a sense that they are very much planted for a secure base to the stroke

46

PUTTING

take dead aim

take dead aim

The aim of the putter is obviously a crucial determining factor in how many putts you make. After all, if you don't aim correctly, how can you be expected to hit your target?

One method that should help you eliminate the likelihood of poor aim is to place the golf ball on the green in such a way that the manufacturer's name corresponds exactly with the line on which you want the ball to start its journey. You should then set the putter-face behind the ball so that it is exactly perpendicular to that line. Alternatively, draw a line on the ball. This is a very effective method, adopted by many of the leading players, because it provides you with a visual image of the perfect aim and path to the hole.

ALIGN THE LOGO

TAKE AIM

47

PUTTING

shoulders and
eyes parallel

shoulders and eyes parallel

Once you have the ideal ball position in your stance, the next key requirement is to have your shoulder-line and eye-line parallel to the path on which you want the ball to start. You can check very easily that these two crucial checkpoints are maintained.

Hold the shaft of the putter along the top of your chest. The line of the shaft should match the target line; if so, it will help promote an on-line stroke.

Also hold the shaft along your eye-line and see if it corresponds with the target line. If so, it further improves your perspective to help you visualize the path the ball must take on its journey to the hole.

SHOULDERS SQUARE

CHECK YOUR EYE LINE

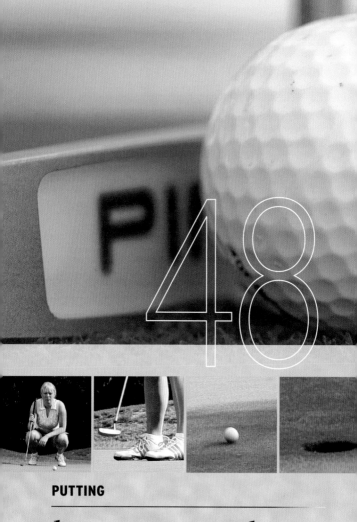

48

how to read greens

how to read greens

No green is totally flat. Thus, most putts have a degree of break on them – often subtle, sometimes severe. The best way to deal with breaking putts and sloping greens is to treat every putt as if it is straight. This is how it works.

■ Identify how much break there is on a putt – for example, a 3ft (90cm) break from the left. The hole itself now ceases to be your target. Your new target is an imaginary hole positioned 3ft (90cm) to the left of the actual hole.

■ As you go through your pre-shot routine, aiming the putter-face and aligning your stance, your focus should continue to be the imaginary target.

■ Now hit a dead-straight putt at your imaginary target to the left of the hole, and the slope on the green takes care of the rest.

The advantage of this method is that you are far more likely to make a pure stroke when hitting a straight putt than you are when trying to guide the ball on a breaking putt.

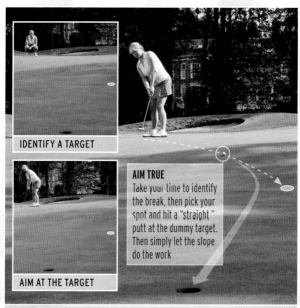

IDENTIFY A TARGET

AIM AT THE TARGET

AIM TRUE
Take your time to identify the break, then pick your spot and hit a "straight" putt at the dummy target. Then simply let the slope do the work

STRIKE A NORMAL PUTT AND LET THE SLOPE DO THE WORK

49

PUTTING

drills

drills

THE PERFECT SHORT-PUTT DRILL

This drill is best practised on a relatively flat portion of the green; the straighter the putt the better.

■ Place your putter on the ground and stick two tee-pegs either side of the heel and toe of the putter-head, leaving about a 1/2 in (1.25cm) gap either side (you can reduce the gap as your confidence grows).

STROKE THROUGH THE PEGS

■ Now place a ball down and simply hit putts, trying to swing the putter-head through the gate formed by the two tee-pegs.

If your stroke is crooked, then either the heel or the toe of the putter will collide with one of the tee-pegs through impact. In this way the drill forces you to make an on-line stroke. If you miss a lot of putts during this practice drill, check the aim of the putter-face at address. It could be that it is not square.

THE PERFECT LONG-PUTT DRILL

One of the best ways to improve your judgement of pace on long putts is to rehearse this practice drill.

■ Place a handful of tee-pegs in the ground, starting at about 20ft (6m) and working away from you at intervals of about 3ft (1m). Use as many tee-pegs as space on the green permits.

■ Now putt the first ball to the first tee-peg, the second ball to the second tee-peg, and so on. The idea is that you get one chance at each putt, just as is the case on the golf course during a real round of golf. You can mix things up a bit, too, by hitting putts randomly to the various tee-pegs.

■ This drill is so effective because it trains you to see a putt and then translate those visual messages into feel for distance.

REFINE YOUR FEEL FOR DISTANCE

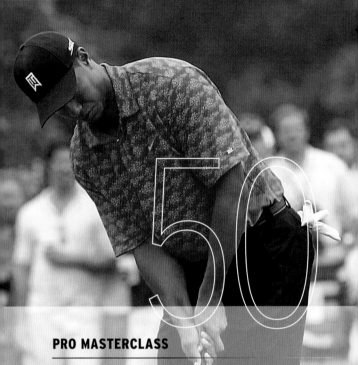

50

Tiger Woods's solid stance

Tiger Woods's solid stance

Next time you watch Tiger Woods putt, ignore for a moment where the ball goes and focus instead on his hips and legs. You will notice that they stay absolutely rock-still throughout the stroke. This is hugely significant and one of the major points of difference between top players and many amateurs.

By keeping the hips and legs steady, Tiger establishes a solid foundation as he swings the putter back and through. It makes it easier to produce an on-line stroke on a more consistent basis, which leads to sweet strikes. This feature of Tiger's putting stroke is well worth copying.

The size of the swing should be in proportion to the length of the putt. Too much swing will result in a loss of accuracy

Woods uses the reverse overlap putting grip. It is thought to be the best way to control the putter

The putter meets the ball on a slight upward arc, imparting a smooth roll

STAY SOLID THROUGH THE STROKE

Success in golf depends a lot less on **strength of body** than upon strength of **mind and character**

ARNOLD PALMER

index

acknowledgments

All images © DK except; **Corbis:** 22/23, 54/55, **Getty Images:** 20/21, 36/37, 38/39, 52/53, 78/79, 106/107, **PA Archive:** 86/87, 92/93

DK would like to thank: Angus Murray and Gerard Brown for photography; Tim Loughead for illustration; Jenny Baskaya for picture research; John Goldsmid and Adam Brackenbury for Creative Technical Support; Richard Gilbert, Ruth O'Rourke, and Clare Weber for editorial assistance; and Margaret McCormack for the index.